SONATAS FOR VIOLIN AND BASSO CONTINUO

Recent Researches in the Music of the Baroque Era is one of four quarterly series (Middle Ages and Early Renaissance, Renaissance, Baroque Era, Classical Era) which make public the early music that is being brought to light in the course of current musicological research.

Each volume is devoted to works by a single composer or in a single genre of composition, chosen because of their potential interest to scholars and performers, and prepared for publication according to the standards that govern the making of all reliable historical editions.

Whenever the demand for works in the series is great enough to warrant the expense, reprints are published for the benefit of performers.

Correspondence should be addressed:

> A-R Editions, Inc.
> Madison, Wisconsin 53703

RECENT RESEARCHES IN THE MUSIC OF THE BAROQUE ERA • VOLUME XI

Jean-Marie Leclair

SONATAS FOR VIOLIN AND BASSO CONTINUO

Opus 5, Opus 9, and Opus 15

Part IV: Opus 9, Sonatas VII–XII
Opus 15, Posthumous Sonata

Edited by Robert E. Preston

A-R EDITIONS, INC. • MADISON

©1971, A-R Editions, Inc.

Contents

Opus 9, Sonatas VII-XII

    Sonata VII   1

    Sonata VIII   17

    Sonata IX   40

    Sonata X   57

    Sonata XI   71

    Sonata XII   85

Opus 15, The Posthumous Sonata   98

SONATAS FOR VIOLIN AND BASSO CONTINUO

Sonata VII

Qui peut se jouer sur la flute allemande

(a) ♪♫ in the source, with the triplet in small notes

(a) The first ending is editorial.

(a) ♩. ♬ in the source, here and in measures 12 and 13

(b) ♩. ♬ in the source

(a) In Leclair's sonatas, an *Altra* such as this is nearly always the mid-portion of a tripartite form, with a *da capo* indicating the return of the movement's opening section. Neither the flute nor the violin version of this movement has a *da capo*, however, and one can only conjecture whether the mark's omission is inadvertent or intentional.

(b) ♩.♬ in the source, here and in measures 16, 17, and 29

(c) ♩.♬ in the source, here and in measure 30

(d) ♩.♬ in the source

(a) ♩♫ in the source

(a) The bowing indications in the first two measures are probably intended to apply to the rest of the movement as well; most unslurred eighth-notes in both violin and continuo should thus be played as though they carried dots.

(a) The first ending is editorial.

Sonata VIII

(a) ![figure] in the source, here and in measures 15, 27, and 57

(a) ♩ ♫♬♬ in the source

(b) This return of the opening theme should probably be played as though it were marked with strokes, as in measures 1-3.

(a) In measures 103-107, the upper notes in the continuo are to be played by the keyboard instrument, the lower notes by the cello or gamba.

26

(a) ♩𝅘𝅥𝅮𝅘𝅥𝅯𝅘𝅥𝅯𝅘𝅥𝅯𝅘𝅥𝅯 in the source

(a) The dots should probably be applied to the remainder of measure 33 and throughout measures 34, 37, and 38.

(a) In measures 73 and 74, ♩♪♪♪♪♪♬ in the source

(a) The continuo should probably be played as though it were marked with strokes, as in measure 237.

(a) Both violin and continuo parts should probably be played as though they were marked with strokes, as in measure 248.

Sonata IX

(a) The movement is actually a French *courante*, not a French *corrente*.

(b) *f* is a quarter-note in the source.

(a) Leclair includes a *segno* and a *custos* but no eighth-note up-beat for the repeat of the first half of the movement; the continuo note *a* has been changed to an eighth to leave room for an up-beat at the end of the measure.

(a) In measures 3 and 4, ♩♪♪♩ in the source

(a) The source's figure, $^6_5$, is incorrect; the violin part suggests that the fifth over the bass should be perfect, not diminished.

Sonata X

(a) In measures 14 and 15, ♪♪. in the source

Sonata XI

75

(a) Measures 130-138 are an editorially written-out *da capo*, repeating measures 1-8 and the first beat of measure 9, which is here supplied with *fermate* as appropriate to the conclusion of the movement.

Sonata XII

(a) [rhythm figure] in the source

(a) ♩. ♫♫ in the source

(a) ⁊ ♫♫ in the source

(b) g″ is a quarter-note in the source.

(c) The second ending is editorial.

88

(a) ![7 notes] in the source

(a) A thirty-second rest in the source, here and at beat 4

(a) The source's curious time-signature is probably either an error or an obscurely humorous way of introducing the movement that closes the fourth book of sonatas. The signature may possibly indicate a kind of proportional puzzle, but the editor is of the opinion that it has no real significance, and that the movement should proceed within a conventional 9/8 framework.

(a) The editor regards as inadvertent the omission of dots on the quarter notes in measures 9 and 10, although the source's notation may suggest some sort of rhythmic distortion, perhaps related to the movement's perplexing time-signature. The editor's conclusion is supported by the fact that all quarter-notes in the movement, apart from those in measures 9 and 10, are dotted.

(b) The "p" seems misplaced; a more likely location is the start of measure 13.

Fine.

Sonata
(The Posthumous Sonata, Opus XV)

(a) ♩♫♩ in the source, here and in measure 46

110